POTATOES

Publications International, Ltd.

Microwave Cooking: Microwave ovens vary in wattage. Use the cooking times as guidelines and check for doneness before adding more time.

Preparation/Cooking Times: Preparation times are based on the approximate amount of time required to assemble the recipe before cooking, baking, chilling or serving. These times include preparation steps such as measuring, chopping and mixing. The fact that some preparations and cooking can be done simultaneously is taken into account. Preparation of optional ingredients and serving suggestions is not included.

WARNING: Food preparation, baking and cooking involve inherent dangers: misuse of electric products, sharp electric tools, boiling water, hot stoves, allergic reactions, foodborne illnesses and the like, pose numerous potential risks. Publications International, Ltd. (PIL) assumes no responsibility or liability for any damages you may experience as a result of following recipes, instructions, tips or advice in this publication.

While we hope this publication helps you find new ways to eat delicious foods, you may not always achieve the results desired due to variations in ingredients, cooking temperatures, typos, errors, omissions, or individual cooking abilities.

Let's get social!
@Publications_International
@PublicationsInternational
www.pilcookbooks.com

TABLE OF CONTENTS

BAKED & ROASTED

SCALLOPED POTATO-ONION BAKE

◇◇◇◇◇◇◇◇◇◇◇◇◇◇◇◇◇◇◇◇◇◇◇◇◇◇◇◇◇◇◇◇◇◇◇◇◇◇

MAKES 6 SERVINGS

1 can (10¾ ounces) CAMPBELL'S® Condensed Cream of Celery Soup (Regular OR 98% Fat Free)

½ cup milk

Dash ground black pepper

4 medium potatoes (about 1¼ pounds), thinly sliced

1 small onion, thinly sliced (about ¼ cup)

1 tablespoon butter, cut into small pieces

Paprika

1. Stir the soup, milk and black pepper in a small bowl. Layer **HALF** the potatoes, onion and soup mixture in a 1½-quart casserole. Repeat the layers. Dot the top with the butter. Sprinkle with the paprika. Cover the baking dish.

2. Bake at 400°F. for 1 hour. Uncover the dish and bake for 15 minutes or until the potatoes are tender.

◇◇◇◇◇◇◇◇◇◇◇◇◇◇◇◇◇◇◇◇◇◇◇◇◇◇◇◇◇◇◇◇◇◇◇◇◇◇

FRESH VEGETABLE CASSEROLE

MAKES 4 TO 6 SERVINGS

8 small new potatoes, unpeeled and halved

8 baby carrots

1 head cauliflower, broken into florets

4 stalks asparagus, cut into 1-inch pieces

3 tablespoons butter

3 tablespoons all-purpose flour

2 cups milk

Salt and black pepper

¾ cup (3 ounces) shredded Cheddar cheese

Chopped fresh cilantro or parsley

1. Preheat oven to 350°F. Grease 2-quart casserole. Steam potatoes, carrots, cauliflower and asparagus in steamer basket over boiling water 5 to 7 minutes or until crisp-tender. Arrange vegetables in prepared casserole.

2. Melt butter in medium saucepan over medium heat. Stir in flour until smooth. Slowly whisk in milk; bring to a boil. Cook and stir 2 minutes or until thickened and bubbly. Season with salt and pepper. Stir in cheese until melted. Pour over vegetables; sprinkle with cilantro.

3. Bake 15 minutes or until heated through.

LITTLE POTATO GRATINS

MAKES 12 GRATINS (6 SERVINGS)

1 cup whipping cream
1 tablespoon fresh thyme
1 clove garlic, minced
1 teaspoon salt
⅛ teaspoon black pepper

2 pounds russet potatoes
¼ cup grated Parmesan cheese
1 cup (4 ounces) grated Gruyère cheese

1. Preheat oven to 375°F. Spray 12 standard (2½-cup) muffin cups with nonstick cooking spray.

2. Pour cream into small microwavable bowl or glass measuring cup. Microwave on HIGH 1 minute or just until cream begins to bubble around edges. Stir in thyme, garlic, salt and pepper until blended; let stand while preparing potatoes.

3. Peel potatoes and cut crosswise into ⅛-inch slices. Layer potato slices in prepared muffin cups, filling half full. Sprinkle with Parmesan; layer remaining potato slices over Parmesan. Pour cream mixture over potatoes; press potato stacks down firmly. Cover pan loosely with foil; place on baking sheet.

4. Bake 30 minutes. Remove pan from oven; sprinkle potatoes with Gruyère. Bake, uncovered, 30 minutes or until potatoes are tender and golden brown. (A paring knife inserted into potatoes should go in easily when potatoes are tender.) Let stand 5 minutes. Use small spatula or knife to loosen edges and bottoms of gratins; remove to plate. Serve warm.

Tip: Gratins can be made ahead, refrigerated and reheated for 10 to 15 minutes in a 350°F oven.

LOADED GRILLED POTATO PACKET

MAKES 4 TO 6 SERVINGS

REYNOLDS WRAP®
Non-Stick Foil

4 medium potatoes, cut into ½-inch cubes

1 large onion, diced

2 tablespoons olive oil

4 slices bacon, cooked and crumbled

2 teaspoons seasoned salt

1 tablespoon chopped fresh chives

1 cup shredded Cheddar cheese

Sour cream (optional)

PREHEAT grill to medium-high or oven to 450°F.

CENTER potatoes and onion on sheet of REYNOLDS WRAP® Non-Stick Foil with non-stick (dull) side toward food. Drizzle with olive oil. Sprinkle with crumbled bacon, seasoned salt, chives and cheese.

BRING up foil sides. Double fold top and ends to seal, making one large foil packet, leaving room for heat circulation inside.

GRILL 18 to 20 minutes in covered grill **OR BAKE** 30 to 35 minutes on a cookie sheet in oven. If desired, serve with sour cream.

POTATO SKINS

8 medium baking potatoes (6 to 8 ounces each), unpeeled

1 tablespoon vegetable oil

1 teaspoon salt

⅛ teaspoon black pepper

1 tablespoon butter, melted

1 cup (4 ounces) shredded Cheddar cheese

8 slices bacon, crisp-cooked and coarsely chopped

1 cup sour cream

3 tablespoons snipped fresh chives

1. Preheat oven to 400°F.

2. Prick potatoes all over with fork. Rub oil over potatoes; sprinkle with salt and pepper. Place in 13×9-inch baking pan. Bake 1 hour or until fork-tender. Let stand until cool enough to handle. *Reduce oven temperature to 350°F.*

3. Cut potatoes in half lengthwise; cut small slice off bottom of each half so potato halves lay flat. Scoop out soft middles of potato skins; reserve for another use. Place potato halves, skin sides up, in baking pan; brush potato skins with butter.

4. Bake 20 to 25 minutes or until crisp. Turn potatoes over; top with cheese and bacon. Bake 5 minutes or until cheese is melted. Cool slightly. Top with sour cream and chives just before serving.

LEMON-DIJON CHICKEN WITH POTATOES

MAKES 6 SERVINGS

2 medium lemons

½ cup chopped fresh parsley

2 tablespoons Dijon mustard

4 cloves garlic, minced

2 teaspoons olive oil

1 teaspoon dried rosemary

¾ teaspoon black pepper

½ teaspoon salt

1 whole chicken (about 3½ pounds)

1½ pounds small red potatoes, unpeeled and halved

1. Preheat oven to 350°F.

2. Squeeze 3 tablespoons juice from lemons; reserve squeezed lemon halves. Combine lemon juice, parsley, mustard, garlic, oil, rosemary, pepper and salt in small bowl; mix well. Reserve 2 tablespoons mixture.

3. Place chicken on rack in shallow roasting pan. Gently slide fingers between skin and meat of chicken breasts and drumsticks to separate skin from meat, being careful not to tear skin. Spoon parsley mixture between skin and meat. (Secure breast skin with toothpicks, if necessary.) Discard any remaining parsley mixture. Place lemon halves in cavity of chicken. Bake 30 minutes.

4. Meanwhile, toss potatoes with reserved parsley mixture in medium bowl until coated. Arrange potatoes around chicken; bake 1 hour or until juices in chicken run clear and thermometer inserted into thickest part of thigh registers 165°F. Remove chicken from oven; let stand 10 minutes. Remove skin; slice chicken. Sprinkle any accumulated parsley mixture from pan over chicken and potatoes.

TRIPLE CHEESE POTATO BAKE

MAKES 8 TO 10 SERVINGS

**REYNOLDS WRAP®
Non-Stick Foil**

2 cans (10¾ ounces each)
reduced-sodium cream of
chicken soup, undiluted

1 container (8 ounces) sour
cream

½ teaspoon black pepper

1 package (30 to 32 ounces)
frozen hash brown
potatoes

¾ cup sliced green onions

1 jar (4 ounces) diced
pimientos, drained

¾ cup shredded sharp
Cheddar cheese

¾ cup shredded Swiss cheese

¼ cup grated Parmesan
cheese

PREHEAT oven to 400°F. Line a 13×9×2-inch baking pan with
REYNOLDS WRAP® Non-Stick Foil with non-stick (dull) side toward
food; set aside.

COMBINE soup, sour cream and pepper in a large bowl; blend
well. Stir in potatoes, onions, pimientos, Cheddar cheese and Swiss
cheese. Spoon into foil-lined pan in an even layer; sprinkle with
Parmesan cheese.

BAKE 45 minutes to 1 hour or until bubbling and golden brown.

SERVE immediately or cool 25 to 30 minutes; cover with non-stick
foil (dull side toward food) and freeze, if desired.

Reynolds Kitchens Tip: To reheat, thaw covered in refrigerator.
Preheat oven to 350°F. Bake 45 minutes to 1 hour or until heated
through. Remove foil after 30 minutes heating time.

HERBED POTATO CHIPS

2 tablespoons minced fresh dill, thyme or rosemary leaves *or* 2 teaspoons dried dill weed, thyme or rosemary

¼ teaspoon garlic salt

⅛ teaspoon black pepper

2 peeled medium red potatoes (about ½ pound)

1 tablespoon olive oil

1¼ cups sour cream

1. Preheat oven to 450°F. Spray baking sheets with nonstick cooking spray. Combine dill, garlic salt and pepper in small bowl; set aside.

2. Cut potatoes crosswise into very thin slices, about ¹⁄₁₆ inch thick. Pat dry with paper towels. Arrange potato slices in single layer on prepared baking sheets; spray potatoes with cooking spray.

3. Bake 10 minutes; turn slices over. Brush with oil; sprinkle evenly with seasoning mixture.

4. Bake 5 to 10 minutes or until golden brown. Cool on baking sheets. Serve with sour cream.

CRISPY OVEN FRIES WITH HERBED DIPPING SAUCE

MAKES 3 SERVINGS

Herbed Dipping Sauce (recipe follows)

2 large unpeeled baking potatoes

2 tablespoons vegetable oil

1 teaspoon kosher salt

1. Preheat oven to 425°F. Line two baking sheets with foil; spray with nonstick cooking spray. Prepare Herbed Dipping Sauce; set aside.

2. Cut potatoes lengthwise into ¼-inch slices, then cut each slice into ¼-inch strips. Combine potato strips and oil on prepared baking sheets. Toss to coat evenly; arrange in single layer.

3. Bake 25 minutes. Turn fries over; bake 15 minutes or until light golden brown and crisp. Sprinkle with salt. Serve immediately with Herbed Dipping Sauce.

Herbed Dipping Sauce: Stir ½ cup mayonnaise, 2 tablespoons chopped fresh herbs (such as basil, parsley, oregano and/or dill), 1 teaspoon salt and ½ teaspoon black pepper in small bowl until smooth and well blended. Cover and refrigerate until ready to serve.

ROAST CHICKEN & POTATOES CATALAN

MAKES 4 SERVINGS

2 tablespoons olive oil

2 tablespoons lemon juice

1 teaspoon dried thyme

½ teaspoon salt

¼ teaspoon ground red pepper

¼ teaspoon ground saffron *or* ½ teaspoon crushed saffron threads or turmeric

2 large baking potatoes (about 1½ pounds), cut into 1½-inch pieces

4 skinless bone-in chicken breasts (about 2 pounds)

1 cup sliced red bell pepper

1 cup frozen peas, thawed

Lemon wedges (optional)

1. Preheat oven to 400°F. Spray large shallow roasting pan or 15×10-inch jelly-roll pan with nonstick cooking spray.

2. Combine oil, lemon juice, thyme, salt, ground red pepper and saffron in large bowl; mix well. Add potatoes; toss to coat.

3. Arrange potatoes in single layer around edges of pan. Place chicken in center of pan; brush both sides of chicken with remaining oil mixture in bowl.

4. Bake 20 minutes. Turn potatoes; baste chicken with pan juices. Add bell pepper; continue baking 20 minutes or until chicken is no longer pink in center, juices run clear and potatoes are browned. Stir peas into potato mixture; bake 5 minutes or until heated through. Garnish with lemon wedges.

MINI TWICE BAKED POTATOES WITH SPICED RAMEN CRISPIES

MAKES 24 PIECES

2 pounds unpeeled small new potatoes, about 1½ to 2 inches in diameter

1 package (8 ounces) cream cheese, softened

1 cup sour cream

1 cup cooked crumbled bacon, divided

½ teaspoon garlic powder

1 teaspoon salt, divided

½ teaspoon black pepper

½ cup (2 ounces) finely shredded sharp Cheddar cheese

¼ cup finely chopped green onions, plus additional for garnish

1 package (3 ounces) ramen noodles, any flavor, crumbled*

1 teaspoon chili powder

½ teaspoon ground cumin

*Discard seasoning packet.

1. Preheat oven to 400°F. Line large baking sheet with foil.

2. Combine potatoes and enough water to cover in Dutch oven; season with salt. Bring to a boil; boil about 10 to 12 minutes or until just tender. Drain and rinse with cold water to cool quickly, shaking off excess liquid.

3. Cut potatoes in half crosswise. Cut thin slice off round end of each potato half to stand upright. Using melon baller or small spoon, scoop out centers of potatoes, leaving ¼-inch-thick shell. Place "meat" of potato in medium bowl. Add cream cheese, sour cream, ½ cup bacon, garlic powder, ½ teaspoon salt and pepper. Mash with potato masher until well combined. Stir in Cheddar cheese and ¼ cup green onions.

4. Sprinkle insides of potato shells with remaining ½ teaspoon salt. Spoon potato mixture evenly into shells.

5. Stir noodles, remaining bacon, chili powder and cumin in medium bowl. Sprinkle evenly over potatoes. Bake 15 to 20 minutes or until lightly browned. Serve sprinkled with additional green onions, if desired.

CREAMY SLAB POTATOES

MAKES 4 SERVINGS

¼ **cup (½ stick) butter, melted**

1 **teaspoon salt**

½ **teaspoon dried rosemary**

½ **teaspoon dried thyme**

¼ **teaspoon black pepper**

2½ **pounds Yukon Gold potatoes, peeled and cut crosswise into 1-inch slices (6 to 8 potatoes)**

1 **cup water**

3 **cloves garlic, smashed**

1. Preheat oven to 500°F.

2. Combine butter, salt, rosemary, thyme and pepper in 13×9-inch baking pan (do not use glass); mix well. Add potatoes; toss to coat. Spread in single layer.

3. Bake 15 minutes. Turn potatoes; bake 15 minutes. Add water and garlic to pan; bake 15 minutes. Remove to serving plate; pour any remaining liquid in pan over potatoes.

FRIED & DEEP FRIED

POTATO-CARROT PANCAKES

MAKES ABOUT 12 PANCAKES

1 pound baking potatoes, peeled (3 medium)

1 medium carrot

2 tablespoons minced green onion

1 tablespoon all-purpose flour

1 egg, beaten

½ teaspoon salt

⅛ teaspoon black pepper

2 tablespoons vegetable oil

Green onion curls (optional)

1. Shred potatoes and carrot. Wrap in several thicknesses of paper towels; squeeze to remove excess moisture.

2. Combine potatoes, carrot, minced green onion, flour, egg, salt and pepper in medium bowl; mix well.

3. Heat oil in large skillet over medium heat. Drop spoonfuls of potato mixture into skillet; flatten to form thin pancakes. Cook 5 minutes or until browned on bottom. Turn pancakes; cook 5 minutes or until potatoes are tender. Garnish with green onion curls.

EXOTIC VEGGIE CHIPS

MAKES ABOUT 6 SERVINGS

Vegetable oil, for deep
   frying

3 tropical tubers (malanga,
   yautia, lila and/or taro
   roots)*

1 to 2 green (unripe)
   plantains

2 parsnips, peeled

1 medium sweet potato,
   peeled

1 lotus root**

Coarse salt

*These tropical tubers are all similar
and their labels are frequently
interchangeable or overlapping. They are
available in the produce section of Latin
markets. Choose whichever tubers are
available and fresh. Look for firm roots
without signs of mildew or soft spots.

**Lotus root is available in the produce
section of Asian markets. The outside
looks like a fat beige link sausage, but
when sliced, the lacy, snowflake-like
pattern inside is revealed.

1. Line baking sheets with paper towels. Fill deep fryer or large
   heavy skillet with oil; heat to 350°F on deep-fry thermometer.

2. Peel thick shaggy skin from tubers, rinse and dry. Thinly slice
   tubers and place in single layer on prepared baking sheets to
   absorb excess moisture. (Stack in multiple layers with paper
   towels between layers.) Peel thick skin from plantain. Slice and
   place on paper towels. Slice parsnips and sweet potato and place
   on paper towels. Trim lotus root and remove tough skin with
   paring knife. Slice and place on paper towels.

3. Working in batches, deep fry each vegetable until crisp and
   slightly curled, stirring occasionally. (Frying time will vary from
   2 to 6 minutes depending on the vegetable.)

4. Remove vegetables with slotted spoon and drain on paper
   towels; immediately sprinkle with salt. Cool completely. Store in
   airtight containers at room temperature.

Note: To recrisp chips, bake in preheated 350°F oven 5 minutes.

SWEET POTATO LATKES WITH CRANBERRY COMPOTE

MAKES 7 SERVINGS

CRANBERRY COMPOTE

1½   cups fresh cranberries
      Peel of 1 orange
½   cinnamon stick
4   peppercorns, cracked
2   whole cloves
½   cup orange juice
¼   cup brandy
⅛   cup packed brown sugar
¼   cup water

LATKES

1   pound uncooked sweet potatoes
2   eggs
¼   cup all-purpose flour
1   small leek, thinly sliced (white part only)
      Salt and black pepper
¼   cup matzo meal
¼   cup canola oil
      Fresh chives (optional)

CRANBERRY COMPOTE

1. Place all ingredients in saucepan over medium-low heat and cook about 25 minutes or until cranberries pop and liquid is slightly reduced. Set aside.

LATKES

2. Peel potatoes and shred using box grater or food processor. Place all ingredients except oil in large bowl and using your hands (a spoon will break up the potato), combine until ingredients are equally distributed.

3. Heat oil in large frying pan over high heat until very hot but not smoking. Flatten about 2 tablespoons batter into pancakes with your hands and gently place in oil. Cook latkes about 2 minutes per side or until browned. Gently remove from oil and place on paper towels to drain.

4. Serve with Cranberry Compote spooned on top of pancakes. Garnish with chives.

CORNED BEEF HASH

2 large russet potatoes, peeled and cut into ½-inch cubes

½ teaspoon salt

¼ teaspoon black pepper

¼ cup (½ stick) butter

1 cup chopped onion

½ pound corned beef, finely chopped

1 tablespoon horseradish

4 eggs

1. Place potatoes in large skillet; add water to cover. Bring to a boil over high heat. Reduce heat to low; simmer 6 minutes. (Potatoes will be firm.) Remove potatoes from skillet; drain well. Sprinkle with salt and pepper.

2. Melt butter in same skillet over medium heat. Add onion; cook and stir 5 minutes. Add corned beef, horseradish and potatoes; mix well. Press mixture with spatula to flatten.

3. Reduce heat to low; cook 10 to 15 minutes. Turn hash in large pieces; pat down and cook 10 to 15 minutes or until bottom is well browned.

4. Meanwhile, bring 1 inch of water to a simmer in small saucepan. Break 1 egg into shallow dish; carefully slide into water. Cook 5 minutes or until white is opaque. Remove with slotted spoon to plate; keep warm. Repeat with remaining eggs.

5. Top each serving of hash with 1 egg. Serve immediately.

FISH & CHIPS

MAKES 4 SERVINGS

¾ cup all-purpose flour

½ cup flat beer or lemon-lime
    carbonated beverage

    Vegetable oil, for frying

4 medium russet potatoes,
    unpeeled and each cut
    into 8 wedges

    Salt

1 egg, separated

1 pound cod fillets (about
    6 to 8 small fillets)

    Malt vinegar (optional)

    Lemon wedges (optional)

1. Combine flour, beer and 2 teaspoons oil in small bowl. Cover
   and refrigerate 1 to 2 hours.

2. Pour 2 inches oil into large heavy skillet; heat to 365°F over
   medium heat. Add potato wedges in batches. (Do not crowd.)
   Fry 4 to 6 minutes or until browned, turning once. (Allow
   temperature of oil to return to 365°F between batches.) Drain
   on paper towels; sprinkle lightly with salt. Reserve oil to fry cod.

3. Stir egg yolk into flour mixture. Beat egg white in medium bowl
   with electric mixer at medium-high speed until soft peaks form.
   Fold egg white into flour mixture.

4. Return oil to 365°F. Dip fish pieces into batter in batches; fry
   4 to 6 minutes or until batter is crispy and brown and fish begins
   to flake when tested with fork, turning once. (Allow temperature
   of oil to return to 365°F between batches.) Drain on paper
   towels. Serve immediately with potato wedges. Sprinkle with
   vinegar and serve with lemon wedges, if desired.

HAM AND POTATO PANCAKES

MAKES 4 SERVINGS (4 PANCAKES EACH)

¾ **pound Yukon Gold potatoes, peeled, grated and squeezed dry (about 2 cups)**

¼ **cup finely chopped green onions**

2 **eggs, beaten**

1 **cup (4 to 5 ounces) finely chopped cooked ham**

¼ **cup all-purpose flour**

¼ **teaspoon salt**

¼ **teaspoon black pepper**

2 **to 3 tablespoons vegetable oil**

Chili sauce or mild fruit chutney (optional)

Green onion curls (optional)

1. Combine grated potatoes, chopped green onions and eggs in large bowl; mix well. Add ham, flour, salt and pepper; mix well.

2. Heat 2 tablespoons oil in large heavy skillet. Drop batter by heaping tablespoonfuls and press with back of spoon to flatten. Cook over medium-high heat 2 to 3 minutes per side. Remove to paper towels to drain. Add remaining 1 tablespoon oil, if necessary, to cook remaining batter. Serve pancakes with chili sauce. Garnish with green onion curls.

CLASSIC HASH BROWNS

MAKES 2 SERVINGS

1 **large russet potato, peeled and grated**

¼ **teaspoon salt**

⅛ **teaspoon black pepper**

2 **tablespoons vegetable oil**

1. Heat medium (8-inch) cast iron skillet over medium heat 5 minutes. Combine potato, salt and pepper in small bowl; toss to coat.

2. Add oil to skillet; heat 30 seconds. Spread potato mixture evenly in skillet. Cook about 5 minutes without stirring or until bottom is browned. Turn potatoes; cook 6 to 8 minutes or until golden brown and crispy.

Ham and Potato
Pancakes

THICK POTATO CHIPS WITH BEER KETCHUP

Beer Ketchup (recipe follows)

1 quart peanut oil

3 unpeeled baking potatoes

Sea salt and black pepper

1. Prepare Beer Ketchup. Heat oil in deep pan to 345°F.

2. Slice potatoes into ¼-inch-thick slices. Lower into oil in batches. Fry 2 minutes per side, flipping to brown evenly on both sides. Drain on paper towels and immediately sprinkle with salt and pepper.

3. Serve with Beer Ketchup.

BEER KETCHUP

MAKES ABOUT 1 CUP

¾ cup ketchup

¼ cup beer

1 tablespoon Worcestershire sauce

¼ teaspoon onion powder

Ground red pepper

Mix all ingredients in small saucepan. Bring to a boil. Reduce heat; simmer 2 to 3 minutes. Remove from heat and let cool. Cover and store in refrigerator until ready to use.

Tip: If the potatoes begin browning too quickly, turn down the heat and wait for the oil to cool to the proper temperature. Too high a temperature will not cook the potatoes completely, and too low a temperature will make the chips soggy.

CHORIZO HASH

2 unpeeled russet potatoes, cut into ½-inch pieces

3 teaspoons salt, divided

8 ounces chorizo sausage

1 yellow onion, chopped

½ red bell pepper, chopped (about ½ cup)

Fried, poached, or scrambled eggs (optional)

Avocado slices (optional)

Fresh cilantro leaves (optional)

1. Fill medium saucepan half full with water. Add potatoes and 2 teaspoons salt; bring to a boil over high heat. Reduce heat to medium-low; cook about 8 minutes. (Potatoes will be firm.) Drain.

2. Meanwhile, remove and discard casing from chorizo. Crumble chorizo into large (12-inch) cast iron skillet; cook and stir over medium-high heat about 5 minutes or until lightly browned. Add onion and bell pepper; cook and stir 4 minutes or until vegetables are softened.

3. Stir in potatoes and remaining 1 teaspoon salt; cook 10 to 15 minutes or until vegetables are tender and potatoes are lightly browned, stirring occasionally. Serve with eggs, if desired; garnish with avocado and cilantro.

CAULIFLOWER POTATO PANCAKES

MAKES 12 PANCAKES (ABOUT 6 SERVINGS)

1½ cups cubed Yukon Gold potatoes, peeled

3 cups roughly chopped cauliflower

⅓ cup whole wheat flour

1 egg, lightly beaten

1 egg white

1 tablespoon chopped fresh chives, plus additional for garnish

1 teaspoon baking powder

½ teaspoon salt

3 teaspoons vegetable oil, divided

Sour cream (optional)

1. Bring large saucepan of water to a boil. Add potatoes and cauliflower; reduce heat. Simmer 10 minutes or until fork-tender. Drain potatoes and cauliflower. Let stand 5 to 10 minutes or until cool enough to handle.

2. Gently mash potatoes and cauliflower in large bowl. Add flour, egg, egg white, 1 tablespoon chives, baking powder and salt; mix well.

3. Heat 1 teaspoon oil in large nonstick skillet over medium heat. Drop ¼ cupfuls potato mixture into skillet; flatten slightly. Cook 5 to 7 minutes per side or until golden brown. Repeat with remaining oil and potato mixture.

4. Serve with sour cream, if desired. Garnish with additional chives.

SAUTÉED GARLIC POTATOES

2 pounds boiling potatoes, peeled and cut into 1-inch pieces

3 tablespoons FILIPPO BERIO® Olive Oil

6 cloves garlic, unpeeled

1 tablespoon lemon juice

1 tablespoon chopped fresh chives

1 tablespoon chopped fresh parsley

Salt and freshly ground black pepper

Place potatoes in large colander; rinse under cold running water. Drain well; pat dry.

In large nonstick skillet, heat olive oil over medium heat until hot. Add potatoes in single layer. Cook, stirring and turning frequently, 10 minutes or until golden brown.

Add garlic. Cover; reduce heat to low and cook very gently, shaking pan and stirring mixture occasionally, 15 to 20 minutes or until potatoes are tender when pierced with fork. Remove garlic; remove and discard skins.

In small bowl, crush garlic; stir in lemon juice. Add to potatoes; mix well. Cook 1 to 2 minutes or until heated through. Transfer to serving dish; sprinkle with chives and parsley. Season to taste with salt and pepper.

BEER-BATTERED SWEET POTATO FRIES AND ONION RINGS WITH LEMON-THYME AIOLI

MAKES 4 TO 6 SERVINGS

Vegetable oil, for frying

2 sweet potatoes (about 6 ounces each), peeled and cut into ¼-inch-thick matchsticks

2 cups all-purpose flour

1½ cups cornstarch

2 teaspoons baking powder

2 tablespoons paprika

1½ teaspoons salt

¼ teaspoon ground red pepper

2 bottles (12 ounces each) lager or other light-colored beer, chilled

1 medium onion (about 12 ounces), cut into ½-inch-thick rounds and separated into individual rings

Lemon-Thyme Aioli (recipe follows)

1. Preheat oven to 200°F. Line large baking sheet with three layers of paper towels. Set lined baking sheet and another baking sheet aside. Fill Dutch oven with 3 inches of oil and heat to 350°F.

2. Place potato pieces in colander and rinse under cold running water. Blot dry with paper towels; set aside.

3. Whisk flour, cornstarch, baking powder, paprika, salt and red pepper in large bowl. Whisk in lager until completely smooth.

4. Place one third of onion rings in batter and mix gently to coat. Remove from batter one at a time, tapping on side of bowl to shake off excess batter before gently dropping into preheated oil. Fry in small batches until golden brown and crisp, 4 to 5 minutes, stirring occasionally so rings don't stick together. Drain on prepared baking sheet, then transfer to another baking sheet and keep warm in oven. Repeat with remaining onion rings.

5. Transfer one fourth of the sweet potatoes to batter and mix gently to coat. Remove from batter a few at a time, tapping on side of bowl to shake off excess batter before gently dropping into preheated oil. Fry in small batches until golden brown and crisp, 7 to 8 minutes, stirring occasionally so fries don't stick together. Transfer to paper towel-lined baking sheet to drain,

then transfer to the oven to keep warm. Repeat with remaining fries. Prepare Lemon-Thyme Aioli. Serve immediately with Lemon-Thyme Aioli for dipping.

LEMON-THYME AIOLI
MAKES ABOUT ½ CUP

- ½ cup mayonnaise
- 1 tablespoon water
- 1 teaspoon finely grated lemon peel
- 2 teaspoons lemon juice
- ¼ teaspoon white pepper
- ½ teaspoon minced fresh thyme
- ⅛ teaspoon minced garlic

Combine all ingredients in small bowl.

MONTEREY POTATO HASH

1 cup cherry tomatoes

2 tablespoons olive oil

4 small baking potatoes, unpeeled and cut into ¼-inch slices

1 medium red onion, sliced

2 cloves garlic, minced

1 teaspoon dried basil or oregano

¼ teaspoon salt

¼ teaspoon black pepper

1 cup water

1 large green bell pepper, halved and cut into ¼-inch slices

¼ cup (1 ounce) shredded Monterey Jack cheese

1. Rinse tomatoes and pat dry with paper towels. Cut tomatoes in half; set aside.

2. Heat wok or large skillet over high heat about 1 minute. Drizzle oil into wok; heat 30 seconds. Add potatoes; cook and stir 8 minutes or until lightly browned. Reduce heat to medium. Add onion, garlic, basil, salt and black pepper; stir-fry 1 minute.

3. Stir in water; cover and cook 5 minutes or until potatoes are fork-tender, gently stirring once. Add bell pepper; stir-fry until water evaporates. Gently stir in tomatoes; cook until heated through. Transfer to serving dish; sprinkle with cheese.

MASHED & SMASHED

ROASTED GARLIC MASHED POTATOES

MAKES 6 TO 8 SERVINGS

REYNOLDS WRAP®
Aluminum Foil

2 **large bulbs garlic**

1 **teaspoon olive oil**

3 **pounds large red potatoes, peeled and cubed**

¼ **cup milk, heated**

¼ **cup (½ stick) butter, softened**

Salt and black pepper

1 **tablespoon chopped fresh parsley**

PREHEAT oven to 400°F. Slice top of bulbs off unpeeled garlic. Remove papery outer layer of garlic bulbs. Place garlic on a sheet of REYNOLDS WRAP® Aluminum Foil. Drizzle with olive oil. Wrap in foil; place on a cookie sheet.

BAKE 25 minutes or until garlic is soft. Cool. Squeeze pulp from garlic and mash in a bowl; set aside.

PLACE potatoes in large saucepan. Cook, covered, in boiling lightly salted water 20 to 25 minutes or until tender. Drain. Mash with potato masher or beat with electric mixer on low speed. Add roasted garlic, milk, butter, salt and pepper to taste. Beat until light and fluffy. Stir in parsley.

MASHED RUTABAGAS AND POTATOES

2 pounds rutabagas, peeled and cut into ½-inch pieces

1 pound potatoes, peeled and cut into ½-inch pieces

½ cup milk

½ teaspoon ground nutmeg

2 tablespoons chopped fresh Italian parsley

Sprigs fresh Italian parsley (optional)

SLOW COOKER DIRECTIONS

1. Place rutabagas and potatoes in slow cooker; add enough water to cover vegetables. Cover; cook on LOW 6 hours or on HIGH 3 hours. Remove vegetables to large bowl using slotted spoon. Discard cooking liquid.

2. Mash vegetables with potato masher. Add milk, nutmeg and chopped parsley; stir until smooth. Garnish with parsley sprigs.

WAFFLED BREAKFAST HASH WITH SMOKED TROUT

1¼ pounds russet potatoes, peeled and cut into ½-inch pieces

½ small red onion, finely diced

1 small red bell pepper, seeded and cut into ½-inch pieces

¼ cup flaked smoked trout

⅓ cup sliced green onions, cut thinly on the bias

2 tablespoons vegetable oil

1 egg, lightly beaten

2 teaspoons cornstarch

½ teaspoon kosher salt

¼ teaspoon black pepper

4 fried eggs, for serving

1. Preheat classic waffle maker to medium-high heat. Set wire rack on large baking sheet.

2. Place potatoes in large saucepan filled with enough water to cover potatoes by 1 inch. Heat to a boil over high heat; reduce heat to medium-low and simmer, partially covered, about 6 to 8 minutes or until tender. Drain potatoes in colander; rinse with cold running water.

3. Place potatoes, onion, bell pepper, trout, green onions, oil, beaten egg, cornstarch, salt and black pepper in large bowl; mix to combine.

4. Place 1 cup potato mixture in center of waffle maker. Close lid firmly; cook about 5 minutes or until waffle is golden brown and crisp. Remove to wire rack; tent with foil to keep warm. Repeat with remaining potato mixture.

5. Serve hash with fried eggs.

BANGERS AND MASH

MAKES 4 TO 6 SERVINGS

- **2** pounds bangers or fresh mild pork sausages
- **2** tablespoons vegetable oil, divided
- **2¼** pounds Yukon Gold potatoes, peeled and cut into 1-inch pieces
- **¾** cup milk, heated
- **3** tablespoons butter, melted
- **1½** teaspoons coarse salt
- **2** small yellow onions, halved and thinly sliced (about 2 cups)
- **1** tablespoon butter
- **1** tablespoon all-purpose flour
- **¼** cup dry red wine
- **1¼** cups beef broth
- Additional salt and black pepper

1. Preheat oven to 400°F. Line baking sheet with foil. Combine sausages and 1 tablespoon oil in large bowl; toss to coat. Place on prepared baking sheet; bake about 20 minutes or until cooked through and golden brown, turning once halfway through cooking.

2. Meanwhile, place potatoes in large saucepan; add water to cover by 2 inches. Bring to a boil over high heat. Reduce heat to medium-low; cook about 12 minutes or until tender. Drain well and press through ricer or mash with potato masher. Stir in warm milk, melted butter and 1½ teaspoons salt until well blended. Set aside and keep warm.

3. Heat remaining 1 tablespoon oil in medium saucepan over medium heat. Add onions; cover and cook about 20 minutes or until caramelized, adding ½ cup water halfway through cooking and stirring occasionally. Add 1 tablespoon butter; cook and stir until melted. Add flour; cook and stir 1 minute. Add wine; cook about 30 seconds or until almost evaporated. Add broth; cook over medium-high heat about 5 minutes or until thickened, stirring occasionally. Season with additional salt and pepper.

4. Serve bangers with mashed potatoes and onion gravy.

MASHED SWEET POTATOES & PARSNIPS

MAKES 6 SERVINGS

2 **large sweet potatoes (about 1¼ pounds), peeled and cut into 1-inch pieces**

2 **medium parsnips (about ½ pound), peeled and cut into ½-inch slices**

¼ **cup evaporated skimmed milk**

1½ **tablespoons butter or margarine**

½ **teaspoon salt**

⅛ **teaspoon ground nutmeg**

¼ **cup chopped fresh chives or green onions**

1. Combine sweet potatoes and parsnips in large saucepan. Cover with cold water; bring to a boil over high heat. Reduce heat; simmer, uncovered, 15 minutes or until vegetables are tender.

2. Drain vegetables; return to pan. Add milk, butter, salt and nutmeg. Mash with potato masher over low heat until desired consistency is reached. Stir in chives.

CRISPY SMASHED POTATOES

MAKES ABOUT 6 SERVINGS

1 tablespoon plus ½ teaspoon salt, divided

3 pounds unpeeled small red potatoes (2 inches or smaller)

4 tablespoons (½ stick) butter, melted, divided

¼ teaspoon black pepper

½ cup grated Parmesan cheese (optional)

1. Fill large saucepan three-fourths full of water; add 1 tablespoon salt. Bring to a boil over high heat. Add potatoes; boil about 20 minutes or until potatoes are tender when pierced with tip of sharp knife. Drain potatoes; set aside until cool enough to handle.

2. Preheat oven to 450°F. Brush baking sheet with 2 tablespoons butter. Working with one potato at a time, smash with hand or bottom of measuring cup to about ½-inch thickness. Arrange smashed potatoes in single layer on prepared baking sheet. Brush with remaining 2 tablespoons butter; sprinkle with remaining ½ teaspoon salt and pepper.

3. Bake 30 to 40 minutes or until bottoms of potatoes are golden brown. Turn potatoes; bake 10 minutes. Sprinkle with cheese, if desired; bake 5 minutes or until cheese is melted.

CREAMY LOADED
MASHED POTATOES

MAKES 8 SERVINGS

3 pounds all-purpose potatoes, peeled and cubed

1½ cups shredded Cheddar cheese (about 6 ounces), divided

1 cup HELLMANN'S® or BEST FOODS® Real Mayonnaise

1 cup sour cream

3 green onions, finely chopped

6 slices bacon or turkey bacon, crisp-cooked and crumbled, divided (optional)

1. Preheat oven to 375°F. Spray 2-quart shallow baking dish with nonstick cooking spray; set aside.

2. Cover potatoes with water in 4-quart saucepot; bring to a boil over high heat. Reduce heat to low and cook 10 minutes or until potatoes are tender; drain and mash.

3. Stir in 1 cup cheese, HELLMANN'S® or BEST FOODS® Real Mayonnaise, sour cream, green onions and 4 slices crumbled bacon. Turn into prepared baking dish and bake 30 minutes or until bubbling.

4. Top with remaining ½ cup cheese and bacon. Bake an additional 5 minutes or until cheese is melted. Garnish, if desired, with additional chopped green onions.

SMASHED POTATOES

4 medium russet potatoes (about 1½ pounds), peeled and cut into ¼-inch cubes

⅓ cup milk

2 tablespoons sour cream

1 tablespoon minced onion

½ teaspoon salt

¼ teaspoon black pepper

⅛ teaspoon garlic powder (optional)

Chopped fresh chives or French fried onions (optional)

1. Bring large saucepan of lightly salted water to a boil. Add potatoes; cook 15 to 20 minutes or until fork-tender. Drain and return to saucepan.

2. Slightly mash potatoes. Stir in milk, sour cream, minced onion, salt, pepper and garlic powder, if desired. Mash until desired texture is reached, leaving potatoes chunky. Cook 5 minutes over low heat or until heated through, stirring occasionally. Top with chives, if desired.

66 MASHED & SMASHED

QUICK MASHED POTATOES WITH CAULIFLOWER

16 ounces russet potatoes, peeled and cut into 2-inch chunks

1 small cauliflower, trimmed into florets (about 4 to 5 cups)

¼ cup water

2 tablespoons vegetable oil spread

2 cloves garlic, minced

½ teaspoon salt

¼ teaspoon black pepper

2 tablespoons chopped fresh chives

1. Place potatoes in medium saucepan; cover with water. Cover; bring to a boil. Reduce heat; simmer 15 minutes or until tender. Drain.

2. Meanwhile, place cauliflower and ¼ cup water in microwavable dish. Cover; microwave on HIGH 5 minutes or until just tender. Drain.

3. Combine potatoes and cauliflower in large bowl. Mash with potato masher. Add vegetable oil spread, garlic, salt and pepper; mix well. Sprinkle with chives.

Note: Adding mashed cauliflower to mashed potatoes cuts down on calories and carbohydrates.

Tip: If you like the texture of the potatoes mashed with a potato masher, but you don't like the graininess of the cauliflower mashed this way, use a hand mixer for the cauliflower before adding the drained potatoes. Then mash with the potato masher.

COLCANNON

6 tablespoons butter, cut into small pieces

3 pounds russet potatoes, peeled and cut into 1-inch pieces

2 medium leeks, white and light green parts only, thinly sliced

½ cup water

2½ teaspoons kosher salt

¼ teaspoon black pepper

1 cup milk

½ small head (about 1 pound) savoy cabbage, cored and thinly sliced

4 slices bacon, crisp-cooked and crumbled

SLOW COOKER DIRECTIONS

1. Sprinkle butter on bottom of slow cooker. Layer half of potatoes, leeks, remaining potatoes, water, salt and pepper. Cover; cook on HIGH 5 hours or until potatoes are tender, stirring halfway through cooking time.

2. Mash potatoes in slow cooker until smooth. Stir in milk and cabbage. Cover; cook on HIGH 30 to 40 minutes or until cabbage is crisp-tender. Stir bacon into potato mixture.

70 MASHED & SMASHED

CHEESY MASHED POTATO WAFFLES

2 cups pre-made or leftover mashed potatoes

1 cup (4 ounces) shredded Cheddar cheese

¼ cup chopped green onions

⅓ cup buttermilk

2 eggs

2 tablespoons butter, melted

½ cup all-purpose flour

1 teaspoon baking powder

½ teaspoon salt

1. Preheat waffle maker to medium.

2. Combine potatoes, cheese, green onions, buttermilk, eggs, butter, flour, baking powder and salt in large bowl; stir well.

3. Scoop 1 cup potato mixture onto waffle maker; spread to cover. Cook about 5 minutes or until golden brown and crisp.

Serving Suggestion: Serve garnished with a dollop of sour cream, shredded cheese and bacon bits.

MASHED POTATOES WITH FRIED ONIONS AND CILANTRO

3 cups cubed (about ½ inch) peeled Yukon Gold potatoes (1 pound total)

1 tablespoon unsalted butter

⅔ cup diced onion

½ cup milk, warmed

2 tablespoons finely chopped fresh cilantro

½ teaspoon salt

¼ teaspoon black pepper

1. Place potatoes in large saucepan; cover with water. Cover; bring to a boil. Reduce heat; boil 15 minutes or until potatoes are tender when pierced with fork.

2. Meanwhile, melt butter in medium nonstick skillet over medium heat. Add onion; cook and stir 7 minutes or until browned.

3. Drain potatoes; return to saucepan. Reduce heat to very low. Stir in milk, onion, cilantro, salt and pepper. Mash with potato masher until smooth and well combined.

SLICED & DICED

WARM POTATO SALAD

MAKES 6 TO 8 SERVINGS

2 pounds fingerling potatoes, unpeeled

3 slices thick-cut bacon, cut into ½-inch pieces

1 small onion, diced

2 tablespoons olive oil

¼ cup cider vinegar

2 tablespoons capers, drained

1 tablespoon Dijon mustard

¾ teaspoon salt

¼ teaspoon black pepper

⅓ cup chopped fresh parsley

1. Place potatoes in large saucepan; add cold water to cover by 2 inches. Bring to a boil over high heat. Reduce heat to medium; cook 10 to 12 minutes or just until potatoes are tender when pierced with tip of small knife.

2. Drain potatoes; let stand until cool enough to handle. Meanwhile, dry out saucepan with paper towels. Add bacon to saucepan; cook until crisp, stirring occasionally. Drain off all but 1 tablespoon drippings.

3. Add onion and oil to saucepan; cook 10 minutes or until onion begins to turn golden, stirring occasionally. Cut potatoes crosswise into ½-inch slices.

4. Add vinegar, capers, mustard, salt and pepper to saucepan; mix well. Remove from heat; stir in potatoes. Add parsley and bacon; stir gently to coat.

SPIRALED SWEET POTATO AND BLACK BEAN TACOS

MAKES 4 SERVINGS

¼ **cup sour cream**

2 **tablespoons mayonnaise**

Juice of 1 lime

½ **teaspoon chipotle chili powder**

1 **can (about 15 ounces) black beans, undrained**

1 **teaspoon smoked paprika**

1 **sweet potato, peeled**

1 **red onion**

1 **green bell pepper**

4 **teaspoons vegetable oil, divided**

¼ **teaspoon salt**

8 **small taco-size tortillas**

1 **avocado, sliced**

¼ **cup chopped fresh cilantro**

¼ **cup grated or shredded cotija cheese**

1. Combine sour cream, mayonnaise, lime juice and chili powder in small bowl; mix well. Refrigerate until ready to use. Combine beans with liquid and paprika in small saucepan. Cook over medium-low heat 5 to 7 minutes or until heated through, stirring occasionally. Remove from heat; coarsely mash beans with potato masher, leaving some beans whole. Keep warm.

2. Spiral sweet potato with medium spiral blade;* cut into desired lengths. Spiral onion with fine spiral blade and bell pepper with spiral slicing blade;* cut into desired lengths.

3. Heat 2 teaspoons oil in medium nonstick skillet over medium heat. Add sweet potato; cook and stir 7 to 10 minutes or until tender. Sprinkle with salt.

4. Heat remaining 2 teaspoons oil in large nonstick skillet over high heat. Add onion and bell pepper; cook and stir 5 minutes or until vegetables are browned and softened.

5. Spread beans down middle of tortillas. Top with sweet potatoes, vegetables, sour cream mixture, avocado, cilantro and cheese; fold in half.

*If you do not have a spiralizer, cut vegetables into thin strips.

POTATO AND LEEK GRATIN

MAKES 6 TO 8 SERVINGS

2 large leeks, sliced

2 pounds baking potatoes, peeled (about 4 medium)

4 tablespoons (½ stick) butter, divided

2 tablespoons minced garlic

2 cups milk

3 eggs

2 teaspoons salt

¼ teaspoon white pepper

2 to 3 slices dense day-old white bread, such as French or Italian

¼ cup grated Parmesan cheese

1. Preheat oven to 375°F. Spray shallow 2½-quart baking dish with nonstick cooking spray. Spiral leeks with spiral slicing blade;* cut into desired lengths. Spiral potatoes with spiral slicing blade; stand potatoes on end and cut in half to form half-moon slices.

2. Melt 2 tablespoons butter in large skillet over medium heat. Add leeks and garlic; cook and stir 8 to 10 minutes or until leeks are softened. Remove from heat.

3. Layer half of potato slices in prepared baking dish; top with half of leek mixture. Repeat layers. Whisk milk, eggs, salt and pepper in medium bowl until well blended; pour evenly over vegetables.

4. Tear bread slices into 1-inch pieces. Place in food processor or blender; process until fine crumbs form. Measure ¾ cup crumbs; place in small bowl. Stir in Parmesan. Melt remaining 2 tablespoons butter; stir into crumb mixture. Sprinkle crumb mixture evenly over vegetables.

5. Bake 1 hour 15 minutes or until top is golden brown and potatoes are tender. Let stand 5 to 10 minutes before serving.

*If you do not have a spiralizer, cut vegetables into thin strips.

VEGETARIAN RICE NOODLES

MAKES 8 SERVINGS

½ cup soy sauce

⅓ cup sugar

¼ cup lime juice

2 fresh red Thai chiles *or* 1 large jalapeño pepper, finely chopped

8 ounces thin rice noodles (rice vermicelli)

2 medium sweet potatoes (1 pound), peeled

1 jicama (8 ounces), peeled

2 large leeks, white and light green parts only

¼ cup vegetable oil

8 ounces firm tofu, drained and cut into triangles

¼ cup chopped unsalted dry-roasted peanuts

2 tablespoons chopped fresh mint, plus additional for garnish

2 tablespoons chopped fresh cilantro

Mint leaves (optional)

1. Combine soy sauce, sugar, lime juice and chiles in small bowl; stir to blend. Set aside.

2. Place rice noodles in medium bowl. Cover with hot water; let stand 15 minutes or until soft. Drain well; cut into 3-inch lengths.

3. Meanwhile, spiral sweet potatoes, jicama and leeks with thin spiral blade;* cut into desired lengths.

4. Heat oil in large skillet over medium-high heat. Add tofu; cook 4 minutes per side or until golden. Remove with slotted spatula to paper towel-lined baking sheet.

5. Add jicama to skillet; stir-fry 5 minutes or until lightly browned. Remove to baking sheet. Stir-fry sweet potatoes in batches until tender and browned; remove to baking sheet. Add leeks; stir-fry 1 minute; remove to baking sheet.

6. Stir soy sauce mixture; add to skillet. Cook and stir until sugar dissolves. Add noodles; toss to coat. Gently stir in tofu, vegetables, peanuts, 2 tablespoons chopped mint and cilantro. Garnish with additional mint.

If you do not have a spiralizer, cut vegetables into thin strips.

SWEET POTATO NACHOS

2 sweet potatoes (1½ pounds total), peeled

1 tablespoon olive oil

Salt and black pepper

1 can (about 15 ounces) black beans, rinsed and drained

1 clove garlic, minced

1 teaspoon ancho or regular chili powder

¼ teaspoon ground chipotle chile (optional)

¼ teaspoon ground cumin

⅛ teaspoon salt

¼ cup water

½ cup (2 ounces) shredded Monterey Jack cheese

Optional toppings: salsa, guacamole, sour cream and chopped green onions

1. Preheat oven to 375°F.

2. Spiral sweet potatoes with spiral slicing blade;* cut slices in half. Place slices in large bowl; drizzle with oil and season with salt and pepper. Toss to coat. Spread on large baking sheet.

3. Bake 30 to 35 minutes or until potatoes are browned and crisp, turning and stirring twice.

4. Meanwhile, cook beans, garlic, chili powder, chipotle, cumin and ⅛ teaspoon salt in small saucepan over medium heat about 3 minutes or until heated through, smashing some beans with spoon and leaving some whole. Stir in water until creamy.

5. Spray 8-inch square baking pan with nonstick cooking spray. Spread bean dip in prepared pan. Arrange sweet potato chips around edges of pan; sprinkle with cheese. Bake 5 minutes or until cheese is melted. Serve with desired toppings.

*If you do not have a spiralizer, cut potatoes into thin slices.

HERBED POT ROAST WITH FINGERLING POTATOES

MAKES 8 SERVINGS

1   boneless beef chuck roast (3 pounds)*

¼   cup all-purpose flour

2   tablespoons olive oil

16   baby carrots

8   fingerling potatoes, unpeeled and halved crosswise

1   medium onion, chopped

2   teaspoons garlic powder

1   teaspoon dried basil

1   teaspoon dried oregano

½   teaspoon dried rosemary

½   teaspoon dried marjoram

½   teaspoon dried sage

½   teaspoon dried thyme

¼   teaspoon black pepper

1½   cups beef broth

Unless you have a 5-, 6- or 7-quart slow cooker, cut any piece of meat larger than 2½ pounds in half so it cooks completely.

SLOW COOKER DIRECTIONS

1. Combine beef and flour in large bowl; toss to coat. Heat oil in large skillet over medium-high heat. Remove beef from flour, reserving flour. Add beef to skillet; cook 6 to 8 minutes or until browned.

2. Meanwhile, add carrots, potatoes, onion, garlic powder, basil, oregano, rosemary, marjoram, sage, thyme and pepper to slow cooker. Combine reserved flour with broth in small bowl; add to slow cooker. Top with beef.

3. Cover; cook on LOW 10 to 12 hours or on HIGH 5 to 6 hours. Remove beef to large cutting board. Cover loosely with foil; let stand 10 to 15 minutes before evenly slicing into eight pieces. Serve with gravy and vegetables.

FARMERS' MARKET POTATO SALAD

MAKES 6 SERVINGS

Pickled Red Onions (recipe follows)

2 pounds assorted potatoes (purple, red, Yukon Gold and/or a combination), unpeeled

1 cup green beans, cut into 1-inch pieces

2 tablespoons plain nonfat Greek yogurt

2 tablespoons white wine vinegar

2 tablespoons olive oil

1 tablespoon spicy mustard

1 teaspoon salt

1. Prepare Pickled Red Onions. Spiral potatoes with spiral slicing blade.* Stand potatoes on end and cut in half into half-moon slices.

2. Bring large saucepan of water to a boil. Add potatoes; cook 4 minutes. Add green beans; cook 2 minutes or until vegetables are fork-tender. Drain and transfer to large bowl. Stir in onions.

3. Stir yogurt, vinegar, oil, mustard and salt in large bowl until smooth and well blended. Pour over vegetables; stir gently to coat. Cover; refrigerate at least 1 hour before serving.

PICKLED RED ONIONS

MAKES ABOUT 1/2 CUP

1 small red onion*

1/4 cup white wine vinegar

2 tablespoons water

1 teaspoon sugar

1 teaspoon salt

1. Spiral red onion with fine spiral blade;* cut into desired lengths.

2. Combine all ingredients in large glass jar. Seal jar; shake well. Refrigerate at least 1 hour or up to 1 week. Recipe can be doubled.

*If you do not have a spiralizer, cut vegetables into thin slices.

CURRIED CAULIFLOWER AND POTATOES

3 tablespoons vegetable oil

1 medium onion, chopped

1 tablespoon minced garlic

1 tablespoon curry powder

1½ teaspoons salt

1½ teaspoons grated fresh ginger

1 teaspoon ground turmeric

1 teaspoon yellow or brown mustard seeds

¼ teaspoon red pepper flakes

1 medium head cauliflower, cut into 1-inch pieces

2 pounds fingerling potatoes, unpeeled and halved

½ cup water

SLOW COOKER DIRECTIONS

1. Heat oil in medium skillet over medium heat. Add onion; cook 8 minutes or until softened. Add garlic, curry powder, salt, ginger, turmeric, mustard seeds and red pepper flakes; cook and stir 1 minute. Remove onion mixture to slow cooker.

2. Stir in cauliflower, potatoes and water. Cover; cook on HIGH 4 hours.

CABBAGE AND RED POTATO SALAD WITH CILANTRO-LIME DRESSING

MAKES 4 SERVINGS

½ **cup finely chopped cilantro**

2 **tablespoons fresh lime juice**

2 **tablespoons olive oil**

2 **teaspoons honey**

½ **teaspoon ground cumin**

¼ **teaspoon salt**

2 **cups sliced napa cabbage**

2 **cups sliced red cabbage**

¾ **pound baby red potatoes (about 4 potatoes), unpeeled, quartered and cooked**

½ **cup sliced green onions**

2 **tablespoons unsalted sunflower kernels**

1. Whisk cilantro, lime juice, oil, honey, cumin and salt in small bowl until smooth and well blended. Let stand 30 minutes to allow flavors to develop.

2. Combine napa cabbage, red cabbage, potatoes and green onions in large bowl; mix well. Add dressing; toss to coat evenly. Sprinkle with sunflower kernels just before serving.

GARDEN POTATO CASSEROLE

1 ¼ **pounds unpeeled baking potatoes, thinly sliced**

1 **green or red bell pepper, thinly sliced**

¼ **cup finely chopped yellow onion**

2 **tablespoons butter, cut into small pieces, divided**

½ **teaspoon dried thyme**
   Salt and black pepper

1 **small yellow squash, thinly sliced**

1 **cup (4 ounces) shredded sharp Cheddar cheese**

SLOW COOKER DIRECTIONS

1. Place potatoes, bell pepper, onion, 1 tablespoon butter and thyme in slow cooker. Season with salt and black pepper; mix well. Layer squash over top; add remaining 1 tablespoon butter.

2. Cover; cook on LOW 7 hours or on HIGH 4 hours.

3. Remove potato mixture to serving bowl. Sprinkle with cheese; let stand 2 to 3 minutes or until cheese is melted.

PESTO ZOODLES WITH POTATOES

MAKES 6 SERVINGS

3 medium red potatoes, peeled

1 large zucchini

¾ cup frozen peas

1 package (about 7 ounces) pesto sauce

¼ cup plus 2 tablespoons grated Parmesan cheese, divided

¼ teaspoon salt

¼ teaspoon black pepper

1. Spiral potatoes and zucchini with fine spiral blade;* cut into desired lengths.

2. Bring medium saucepan of water to a boil. Add potatoes; cook 5 to 7 minutes or until tender, adding peas and zucchini during last 2 minutes of cooking. Drain well; return to saucepan. Stir in pesto, ¼ cup cheese, salt and pepper, tossing until blended.

3. Sprinkle with remaining 2 tablespoons cheese just before serving.

*If you do not have a spiralizer, cut vegetables into thin strips.

CREAMY RED POTATO SALAD

3 pounds red bliss or new potatoes, cut into ¾-inch chunks

½ cup WISH-BONE® Italian Dressing*

¾ cup HELLMANN'S® or BEST FOODS® Real Mayonnaise

½ cup sliced green onions

1 teaspoon Dijon mustard

1 teaspoon lemon juice

⅛ teaspoon ground black pepper

*Also terrific with WISH-BONE® Robusto Italian or House Italian Dressing.

1. Cover potatoes with water in 4-quart saucepot; bring to a boil over medium-high heat. Reduce heat to low and simmer 10 minutes or until potatoes are tender. Drain and cool slightly.

2. Combine all ingredients except potatoes in large salad bowl. Add potatoes and toss gently. Serve chilled or at room temperature.

BOILED & BLENDED

LEMON-MINT RED POTATOES

MAKES 4 SERVINGS

2 pounds unpeeled new red potatoes

3 tablespoons olive oil

1 teaspoon salt

¾ teaspoon Greek seasoning or dried oregano

¼ teaspoon garlic powder

¼ teaspoon black pepper

4 tablespoons chopped fresh mint, divided

2 tablespoons butter

2 tablespoons lemon juice

1 teaspoon grated lemon peel

SLOW COOKER DIRECTIONS

1. Coat 6-quart slow cooker with nonstick cooking spray. Add potatoes and oil; toss to coat. Sprinkle with salt, Greek seasoning, garlic powder and pepper. Cover; cook on LOW 7 hours or on HIGH 4 hours.

2. Stir in 2 tablespoons mint, butter, lemon juice and lemon peel until butter is completely melted. Cover; cook on HIGH 15 minutes to allow flavors to blend. Sprinkle with remaining 2 tablespoons mint just before serving.

Tip: Potatoes can stand at room temperature, covered, for up to 2 hours.

POTATO CHEDDAR SOUP

MAKES 6 SERVINGS

2 pounds new red potatoes, unpeeled and cut into ½-inch pieces

3 cups chicken or vegetable broth

1 medium onion, coarsely chopped

¾ cup coarsely chopped carrots

½ teaspoon salt

1 cup half-and-half

¼ teaspoon black pepper

2 cups (8 ounces) shredded Cheddar cheese

Seasoned croutons (optional)

SLOW COOKER DIRECTIONS

1. Place potatoes, broth, onion, carrots and salt in slow cooker. Cover; cook on LOW 6 to 7 hours or on HIGH 3 to 3½ hours or until vegetables are tender.

2. Stir in half-and-half and pepper. Cover; cook on HIGH 15 minutes. Turn off heat. Let stand, uncovered, 5 minutes. Stir in cheese until melted. Top with croutons, if desired.

POTATO HERB SOUP

MAKES 5 SERVINGS

2 cups Southern-style frozen hash brown potatoes

1½ cups sliced frozen carrots

2 tablespoons SPICE ISLANDS® Minced Onion

1 can (14½ ounces) chicken or vegetable broth

1 cup water

½ teaspoon SPICE ISLANDS® Sweet Basil

½ teaspoon SPICE ISLANDS® Garlic Salt

¼ teaspoon SPICE ISLANDS® Ground Coriander

¼ teaspoon SPICE ISLANDS® Fine Grind Black Pepper

⅛ teaspoon SPICE ISLANDS® Cayenne Pepper

1 cup half and half

2 tablespoons butter or margarine

COMBINE potatoes, carrots, onion, broth, water, basil, garlic salt, coriander, black pepper and cayenne pepper in a large saucepan. Cover; bring to boil. Reduce heat.

SIMMER 5 minutes or until potatoes and carrots are tender. Add half and half and butter; heat through.

SWEET POTATO & PECAN SOUP

MAKES 8 SERVINGS

- **2 tablespoons unsalted butter**
- **1 large sweet onion, coarsely chopped (about 2 cups)**
- **4 cloves garlic, minced**
- **6 cups SWANSON® Chicken Broth (Regular, Natural Goodness® OR Certified Organic)**
- **2 bay leaves**
- **¼ teaspoon ground black pepper**
- **3 large sweet potatoes, peeled and cut into cubes (about 6 cups)**
- **1 cup heavy cream**
- **3 tablespoons thinly sliced fresh chives**
- **1 cup pecans, toasted and chopped**
- **Chive Chantilly**

1. Heat the butter in a 6-quart saucepot over medium heat. Add the onions and garlic and cook until the onions are tender.

2. Add the broth, bay leaves, black pepper and potatoes. Heat to a boil. Reduce the heat to low. Cover and cook for 20 minutes or until the potatoes are tender. Discard the bay leaves.

3. Add ½ **CUP** of the cream and heat through.

4. Place ⅓ of the broth mixture into a blender or food processor. Cover and blend until smooth. Pour the mixture into a large bowl. Repeat the blending process twice more with the remaining broth mixture. Return all of the puréed mixture to the saucepot. Cook over medium heat for 5 minutes or until hot. Season to taste.

5. Prepare the *Chive Chantilly*. Serve the soup with *Chive Chantilly* and sprinkle with pecans.

Chive Chantilly: Beat the remaining heavy cream in a medium bowl with an electric mixter on high speed until stiff peaks form. Gently stir in the chives.

Tip: It's best to toast nuts whole first and then chop them. Spread the pecans in a single layer on a jelly-roll pan. Bake at 300°F. for 15 minutes or until the pecans are toasted. Cool and use as directed above.

POTATO AND LEEK SOUP

MAKES 6 TO 8 SERVINGS

4 cups chicken broth

3 potatoes, peeled and diced

1½ cups chopped cabbage

1 leek, diced

1 onion, chopped

2 carrots, diced

1 teaspoon salt

½ teaspoon caraway seeds

½ teaspoon black pepper

1 bay leaf

½ cup sour cream

1 pound bacon, crisp-cooked and crumbled

¼ cup chopped fresh parsley

SLOW COOKER DIRECTIONS

1. Combine broth, potatoes, cabbage, leek, onion, carrots, salt, caraway seeds, pepper and bay leaf in slow cooker; mix well.

2. Cover; cook on LOW 8 to 10 hours or on HIGH 4 to 5 hours.

3. Remove and discard bay leaf. Whisk ½ cup hot liquid from slow cooker into sour cream in small bowl until blended. Add sour cream mixture and bacon to slow cooker; mix well. Sprinkle with parsley.

APPLE, TATER & CARROT JUICE

MAKES 4 SERVINGS

4 **apples**
1 **sweet potato**

1 **carrot**

Juice apples, sweet potato and carrot. Stir.

BACK TO YOUR ROOTS

MAKES 3 SERVINGS

2 **beets**
2 **carrots**
2 **parsnips**

1 **turnip**
1 **sweet potato**

Juice beets, carrots, parsnips, turnip and sweet potato. Stir.

Apple, Tater &
Carrot Juice

COUNTRY CHICKEN CHOWDER

MAKES 4 SERVINGS

1   pound chicken tenders

2   tablespoons butter

1   small onion, chopped

1   stalk celery, sliced

1   small carrot, sliced

1   can (10¾ ounces)
    condensed cream of
    potato soup, undiluted

1   cup milk

1   cup frozen corn

½   teaspoon dried dill weed

    Salt and black pepper

1. Cut chicken tenders into ½-inch pieces.

2. Melt butter in large saucepan or Dutch oven over medium-high heat. Add chicken; cook and stir 5 minutes.

3. Add onion, celery and carrot; cook and stir 3 minutes. Stir in soup, milk, corn and dill weed; reduce heat to low. Cook about 8 minutes or until corn is tender and chowder is heated through. Season with salt and pepper.

Tip: For a special touch, garnish soup with croutons and fresh dill. For a hearty winter meal, serve the chowder in hollowed-out toasted French rolls or small round sourdough loaves.

PASTA & POTATOES WITH PESTO

MAKES 6 SERVINGS

3 medium red potatoes, unpeeled and cut into 1-inch pieces

8 ounces uncooked linguine

¾ cup frozen peas

1 package (about 7 ounces) prepared pesto sauce

¼ cup plus 2 tablespoons grated Parmesan cheese, divided

¼ teaspoon salt

¼ teaspoon black pepper

1. Place potatoes in medium saucepan; cover with water. Bring to a boil over high heat; reduce heat. Cook, uncovered, 10 minutes or until potatoes are tender; drain.

2. Meanwhile, cook linguine according to package directions, adding peas during last 3 minutes of cooking; drain. Return pasta mixture to saucepan; add potatoes, pesto sauce, ¼ cup cheese, salt and pepper, tossing until blended.

3. Sprinkle with remaining 2 tablespoons cheese.

HEARTY CORN, CHILE AND POTATO SOUP

2 tablespoons butter

2 stalks celery, sliced

1 medium onion, coarsely chopped

2½ cups water

2 cups diced potatoes

1 can (14.75 ounces) cream-style corn

1 can (11 ounces) whole-kernel corn, undrained

1 can (4 ounces) ORTEGA® Fire-Roasted Diced Green Chiles

2 chicken bouillon cubes

1 teaspoon paprika

1 bay leaf

1 can (12 ounces) evaporated milk

2 tablespoons flour

Salt and black pepper, to taste

MELT butter in large saucepan over medium-high heat. Add celery and onion; cook for 1 to 2 minutes or until onion is tender. Add water, potatoes, corn, chiles, bouillon, paprika and bay leaf. Bring to a boil. Reduce heat to low; cover.

COOK, stirring occasionally, for 15 minutes or until potatoes are tender. Stir a small amount of evaporated milk into flour in small bowl to make a smooth paste; gradually stir in remaining milk. Stir milk mixture into soup. Cook, stirring constantly, until soup comes just to a boil and thickens slightly. Season with salt and pepper.

LOADED BAKED POTATO SOUP

MAKES 6 TO 8 SERVINGS (8 CUPS)

3   medium russet potatoes
    (about 1 pound)
¼   cup (½ stick) butter
1   cup chopped onion
½   cup all-purpose flour
4   cups chicken or vegetable
    broth
1½ cups instant mashed
    potato flakes
1   cup water
1   cup half-and-half

1   teaspoon salt
½   teaspoon dried basil
½   teaspoon dried thyme
¼   teaspoon black pepper
1   cup (4 ounces) shredded
    Cheddar cheese
4   slices bacon, crisp-cooked
    and crumbled
1   green onion, chopped

1. Preheat oven to 400°F. Scrub potatoes and prick in several places with fork. Place in baking pan; bake 1 hour. Cool completely; peel and cut into ½-inch cubes. (Potatoes can be prepared several days in advance; refrigerate until ready to use.)

2. Melt butter in large saucepan or Dutch oven over medium heat. Add onion; cook and stir 3 minutes or until softened. Whisk in flour; cook and stir 1 minute. Gradually whisk in broth until well blended. Stir in mashed potato flakes, water, half-and-half, salt, basil, thyme and pepper; bring to a boil over medium-high heat. Reduce heat to medium; cook 5 minutes.

3. Stir in baked potato cubes; cook 10 to 15 minutes or until soup is thickened and heated through. Ladle into bowls; top with cheese, bacon and green onion.

SWEET POTATO SHEPHERD'S PIE

MAKES 6 SERVINGS

1 large sweet potato, peeled and cubed

1 large russet potato, peeled and cubed

½ to 1 cup milk

1½ teaspoons salt, divided

2 cups chicken broth

3 tablespoons rice flour

1 teaspoon cider vinegar

1 teaspoon dried thyme

½ teaspoon dried sage

½ teaspoon black pepper

1 pound ground turkey

2 packages (4 ounces each) sliced mixed mushrooms *or* 8 ounces sliced cremini mushrooms

1 tablespoon minced garlic

¾ cup frozen baby peas, thawed

1. Place potatoes in medium saucepan. Cover with water; bring to a boil over medium-high heat. Reduce heat; cover and simmer 20 minutes or until potatoes are very tender. Drain potatoes; return to saucepan. Mash with potato masher; stir in enough milk until desired consistency is reached and ½ teaspoon salt.

2. Heat broth in small saucepan over medium heat. Whisk in rice flour; cook and stir 2 minutes. Reduce heat to low; cook until thickened. Stir in vinegar, thyme, remaining 1 teaspoon salt, sage and pepper.

3. Spray large nonstick ovenproof skillet with nonstick cooking spray. Add turkey, mushrooms and garlic; cook and stir over medium-high heat until turkey is no longer pink and mushrooms begin to give off liquid.

4. Pour gravy into skillet; simmer 5 minutes. Add peas; cook and stir until heated through. Remove from heat. Spoon potato mixture over turkey mixture; spray with cooking spray.

5. Preheat broiler. Broil 4 to 5 inches from heat source 5 minutes or until mixture is heated through and potatoes begin to brown.

BAKED POTATO SOUP

3 cans (10¾ ounces each) condensed cream of mushroom soup

4 cups milk

3 cups diced peeled baked potatoes

½ cup cooked crumbled bacon

1 tablespoon fresh thyme leaves or 1 teaspoon dried thyme leaves

Sour cream and shredded Cheddar cheese

1½ cups FRENCH'S® French Fried Onions

1. Combine soup and milk in large saucepan until blended. Stir in potatoes, bacon and thyme. Cook over medium heat about 10 to 15 minutes or until heated through, stirring frequently. Season to taste with salt and pepper.

2. Ladle soup into serving bowls. Top each serving with sour cream, cheese and 3 tablespoons French Fried Onions.

INDEX

ACKNOWLEDGMENTS

The publisher would like to thank the companies listed below for the use of their recipes and photographs in this publication.

ACH Food Companies, Inc.
Campbell Soup Company
Filippo Berio® Olive Oil
Unilever
Reckitt Benckiser LLC.

Recipes courtesy of the Reynolds Kitchens
Pinnacle Foods
Ortega®, A Division of B&G Foods North America, Inc.

METRIC CONVERSION CHART

VOLUME MEASUREMENTS (dry)

1/8 teaspoon = 0.5 mL
1/4 teaspoon = 1 mL
1/2 teaspoon = 2 mL
3/4 teaspoon = 4 mL
1 teaspoon = 5 mL
1 tablespoon = 15 mL
2 tablespoons = 30 mL
1/4 cup = 60 mL
1/3 cup = 75 mL
1/2 cup = 125 mL
2/3 cup = 150 mL
3/4 cup = 175 mL
1 cup = 250 mL
2 cups = 1 pint = 500 mL
3 cups = 750 mL
4 cups = 1 quart = 1 L

VOLUME MEASUREMENTS (fluid)

1 fluid ounce (2 tablespoons) = 30 mL
4 fluid ounces (1/2 cup) = 125 mL
8 fluid ounces (1 cup) = 250 mL
12 fluid ounces (1 1/2 cups) = 375 mL
16 fluid ounces (2 cups) = 500 mL

WEIGHTS (mass)

1/2 ounce = 15 g
1 ounce = 30 g
3 ounces = 90 g
4 ounces = 120 g
8 ounces = 225 g
10 ounces = 285 g
12 ounces = 360 g
16 ounces = 1 pound = 450 g

DIMENSIONS

1/16 inch = 2 mm
1/8 inch = 3 mm
1/4 inch = 6 mm
1/2 inch = 1.5 cm
3/4 inch = 2 cm
1 inch = 2.5 cm

OVEN TEMPERATURES

250°F = 120°C
275°F = 140°C
300°F = 150°C
325°F = 160°C
350°F = 180°C
375°F = 190°C
400°F = 200°C
425°F = 220°C
450°F = 230°C

BAKING PAN SIZES

Utensil	Size in Inches/Quarts	Metric Volume	Size in Centimeters
Baking or Cake Pan (square or rectangular)	8×8×2	2 L	20×20×5
	9×9×2	2.5 L	23×23×5
	12×8×2	3 L	30×20×5
	13×9×2	3.5 L	33×23×5
Loaf Pan	8×4×3	1.5 L	20×10×7
	9×5×3	2 L	23×13×7
Round Layer Cake Pan	8×1½	1.2 L	20×4
	9×1½	1.5 L	23×4
Pie Plate	8×1¼	750 mL	20×3
	9×1¼	1 L	23×3
Baking Dish or Casserole	1 quart	1 L	—
	1½ quart	1.5 L	—
	2 quart	2 L	—